# A different kind of city

Bucharest is not a single city but several, jumbled together in a curious assortment, each oblivious to the others. To the eye more used to western cities, to the spirit shaped by an approach to town planning based on a hunger for every possible square centimetre of space, Bucharest is an unusual place, to say the least.

A city of paradoxes and contrasts, rising up in the middle of a seemingly infinite plain, Bucharest is a splendid chaos.

The city's extraordinary variety makes it seem like the marvellous product of an aesthetic storm: no two houses, no two structures are alike. Buildings in the cubist style leap up alongside imposing neo-Romanian edifices. Thatched cottages made of packed earth, hidden beneath trailing bunches of wisteria, survive discreetly and charmingly in the shade of a colonnaded neo-classical building in red marble. The elegance of a little old church, carefully ornamented with stucco bas-reliefs darkened by the weather, contrasts with solemn, monumental constructions bearing the marks of French academism or the neo-Gothic style.

But little by little, this enormous palace built by a megalomaniac dictator and the new quarter surrounding it take their place in this 'normality' which is so characteristic of Bucharest. The churches and monasteries hidden piously on either side of the great boulevard dividing this quarter ensure that the present urban 'integration' takes place in spite of any reservations.

The city's unique character lies in this amazing, spectacular and colourful combination of incompatible buildings, this obsession with diversity.

*1. The statue of the She-wolf 'Lupoaica' and the Patriarchate Hill in the 30s.*

*2. Two worlds in close contact: horse-drawn cart and a Mercedes in Bucharest.*

*3. Beautiful Wallachian girls…*

---

\* Extract from the address given by Raymond Poincaré (1860–1934) – President of the Republic of France between 1913 and 1920 – to an international hearing held in Bucharest after the First World War (cf. the epigraph to a famous Romanian novel from between the wars, *"Craii de Curtea-Veche"* by Mateiu Caragiale).

Bucharest is a strange city which you may love, hate, even despise, but which will never leave you unmoved.

Everyone can invent his or her own Bucharest, in the same way that all lovers claim the stars in the sky for their own.

4

5

Those who dream of the clean and comfortable magic of elegant villas and residential gardens will find real gems of modern European architecture beneath the chestnut and lime trees of the Cotroceni and Dorobanti quarters.

But be careful! If you give yourself too freely to the shadows of the night and the intoxicating scent of the limes, you may suddenly realise that you have passed a 'frontier' no broader than a street, and that you are now 'on the other side of the fence', in the most authentic and picturesque gipsy quarter.

Once you have had your fill of the roar of the great Maghéru boulevard with its high buildings and its precise, energetic architectural style, let yourself be taken eastwards along a real road such as the Eminescu or the Batistei. This is where you will find fantasy at its most voluptuous and fertile, with originality as the first principle. You will never find two houses the same in this charming, motley clutter.

An encounter with Bucharest cannot be hurried. If the city is accustomed to tumultuous changes, to sudden metamorphoses in the wake of floods or earthquakes, this is partly due to the temperament of the inhabitants themselves. Behind their restless, impatient, perpetual agitation, there lies a serene contemplation and watchfulness which they have succeeded in breathing into their city.

It is best to put aside your map and discover the city for yourself, guided by chance and intuition. Bucharest is surprising and picturesque at every step, so wander where you will. Let yourself be filled for a few hours with the oriental, easy-going air which infuses this splendid city. Lombard cable mouldings are provocatively contrasted with sensual and anachronistic arabesques. Round Byzantine arches, shaped like the handles of bread-baskets, recite cheerful soliloquies to sombre and mysterious elongated ogives. Armenian pediments, neo-classical colonnades, Russian cupolas, Venetian loggias and neo-Wallachian verandahs are intermingled everywhere.

\* \* \* \* \*

Walking is really the only way to experience this city awash with flowers, trees and gardens, surrounded by lakes, parks and forests.

7. *The Stavropoleos church in 1862: painting by H. Trenk.*

8. *The Stavropoleos church (the entrance open hall): an exceptional monument of brâncovenesc style (1724), restored in 1904 by the leader of the Romanian architecture school, Ion Mincu.*

8

9. *The ARO building (show room, bar, offices) in the 30s: built in the 30s, according to plans drawn up by architect Horia Creanga.*

10. *The Bucur church: built in the 18th century; according to legend, it might be connected to the foundation of Bucharest.*

# A little history

Bucharest's origins as a medieval fortress built in the midst of the surrounding Wallachian villages are lost in the mists of the Danubian plain. Compared with those of the great cities founded in the Middle Ages, its monuments are still damp with the ink of history.

Bucharest is still a young city, built in the 15th century and destined to become a market town, a commercial intermediary at the crossroads of the great European trade routes and a kind of turntable between East and West, in an area both accessible and prosperous.

There is a legend, much loved by the people of Bucharest, which tells of a visionary founder, a shepherd named Bucur who is said to have built a house here, or perhaps a church. The present Bucur church, which is somewhat rustic in appearance, actually dates from the late 18th century. But the mythical elements in the story of the city's foundation support a hypothesis currently championed by several experts concerning the sacred character of the medieval structure of Bucharest. According to this theory, the city developed in a measured, concentric progression which followed the siting of its churches and monasteries in a kind of celestial geometry.

A surviving document dated 20 September 1459, issued by the Wallachian chancellery of Vlad the Impaler – the legendary Prince Dracula (to use his patronymic, which in Romanian means 'the devil') – does not mention the very birth of Bucharest, but it does allude to the existence of a citadel on the banks of the Dâmbovitza river.

\* \* \* \* \*

The Wallachian princes – the last European crusaders, and the new protectors of the people and Christian saint-places of the Balkans after the fall of Constantinople in 1453 – were the last bastion of Christianity against the rise of the Ottoman empire.

In less than a century, Bucharest became an important cultural centre, a shining light for the orthodox East. A magnificent princely court, known as *Curtea Domneasca* (later renamed *Curtea Veche* – 'The Old Court') was established on the left bank of the Dâmbovitza around the middle of the 16th century.

During the two-and-a-half centuries following the fall of Constantinople – known to historians as the 'post-Byzantine' period – numerous churches and monasteries of great beauty were built in and around the city.

The 17th century witnessed a veritable cultural Renaissance in the Romanian principalities. In Wallachia in particular, Romanian art attained a peak of vitality, successfully assimilating forms from many different sources.

Two periods are especially notable for their remarkable fertility. The reign of the builder prince Matei Basarab (1632–1654) was the most dynamic era in the history of Romanian ecclesiastical architecture. One of the distinctive elements of religious architecture of this period is the open *exonartex* (entrance vestibule) supported on pillars; this feature is very characteristic of Wallachian architecture, and recurs in buildings of the succeeding period. A notable legacy of this era is the fortified monastery of Caldarusani, in the north of the city, which provided military protection to the capital.

Wallachian art reached its peak in the late 17th and early 18th centuries in the reign of Prince Brâncoveanu (1688–1714). The numerous buildings he commissioned have a characteristic style which now bears his name, a synthesis of Renaissance and Baroque elements grafted on to the old local artistic traditions. Similarly, the religious architecture uses carved stone in forms borrowed from the Baroque style; this new form of sculpture also adorns the palaces, which successfully introduced elements both western (loggia) and eastern into structures which nevertheless conformed to tradition.

The Church of Coltea dates from this period. It used to be devoted to the oldest hospital in Bucharest, and it lies diagonally opposite the present University building. Another little marvel, the Stavropoleos church – built somewhat later (1724) between *Curtea Veche* and the Lipscani commercial street – has the same 'brâncovenesque' style. In the north of the city, the prince commissioned the building of a magnificent residence, the Mogosoaia Palace.

A road was built during Brâncoveanu's reign to link the prince's court in Bucharest to his Mogosoaia Palace. The 'intra muros' section of this road became known as 'Mogosoaia Bridge' (*Podul Mogosoaiei*), and was given a covering of oak joists. The history of this road is that of the city itself. In 1878 the 'bridge' was proudly renamed 'Victory Avenue' (*Calea Victoriei*) to mark Romania's newly-won independence

* * * * *

At the beginning of the 18th century, the Turkish sultans replaced the Romanian princes – tireless defenders of the Christian world – with foreigners, rich Greeks originally from Phanar, a quarter of Istanbul. The so-

*11. The Antim monastery (inner courtyard): the most coherent monastic ensemble of the city.*

*12. The church of the Antim monastery: built in 1713 by the scholar mitropolite, Antim Ivireanul.*

called 'phanariotes' were to hold the country's throne for more than a century.

At this time, there were several inns on the left bank of the Dimbovita, not far from *Curtea Domneasca* and the commercial quarter of the city. *Hanul Manuc,* an inn built immediately opposite the Court in the early 19th century, is one of the few 'phanariote' buildings which have survived the ravages of time, a 'caravanserai' intelligently restored and used as a hotel and restaurant. Not far away, *Hanul cu Tei* ('Lime-tree Inn') has also been tastefully transformed into a huge exhibition space for art shows and a marketplace for secondhand booksellers.

The quarter around the Princely Court was effectively a permanent fair, a kind of huge bazaar. The alleyways – organised according to the various types of trades – were covered with fir branches, rather like Mogosoaia Bridge – hence the name *'târg învelit'* ('covered fair') given to the quarter.

The best-known merchants were the 'lipscani', traders who, during the 18th century, would travel twice a year to the great German fair in Leipzig.

In 1776, for security reasons, the 'phanariote' princes decided to move their headquarters to the hill in the centre of the town. Here they built the new Princely Court, on whose ruins the present Parliament Palace now stands.

\* \* \* \* \*

At the beginning of the 19th century, Bucharest had a population of some 70,000 inhabitants.

There was a 'resolute, spontaneous and almost passionate return to the West' in Wallachia immediately after 1821, a year of major national upheavals in the Balkan region. Modern Romania (comprising Wallachia and Moldavia) won its independence in 1877 and became a kingdom in 1881. The capital was modernised in a frenzy of eagerness to assimilate western civilization. The 'French model' acquired authority and soon became the prevailing influence, the only template to be followed: Bucharest changed according to the trends in Parisian architecture and lifestyle. *"In no other part of Europe would the French influence be so profound or so prolonged as in the Romanian Principalities"* (Neagu Djuvara). From the early 19th century until the inter-war period, the Romanian people maintained a very close relationship with France, a 'passionate affair', as Helene Vacarescu – the Romanian poet writing in French – has put it. According to the 'French myth', Romania turned itself into 'the Belgium of the East' in order to get closer to its great Latin sister, France.

14

A large part of the city was destroyed by a disastrous fire in 1847. In 1860, urban renewal plans began to be drawn up according to the principles established by Baron Haussmann, creator of the celebrated Parisian boulevards.

Before long, a first great boulevard extended the thoroughfare running alongside the University and the Cismigiu Gardens, spreading both westwards and eastwards. At the beginning of the following century, a new western section was built to connect with the Cotroceni residential quarter.

Central Bucharest was gradually transformed into something like a western city, perhaps a French city. But the parallel is only approximate, since the new buildings constructed by French and Romanian architects, although imbued with the Parisian academic aestheticism of the late 19th-century Ecole des Beaux-Arts, were grafted on to the characteristic unruliness of the old city. The architectural historicism of this period resulted in the eclectic co-existence of several 'neo' styles (neo-classical, neo-Renaissance, neo-Gothic), sometimes all in the same building.

The Dâmbovitza river was tamed into the form of a canal. Modern infrastructures such as a sewage system, electric street lighting and tramways began to form part of the urban landscape around 1900, and became more firmly established during subsequent decades.

Bucharest became illuminated by the light of the West.

* * * * *

During the last years of the 19th century and the first two decades of the 20th, a new wave of creativity swept over the city. 'La Belle Epoque' prompted Romanians to find new pride in a national style, itself born of an innovative mixture of styles – the native 'brâncovenesque' and European Art Nouveau. Romanian architects (Ion Mincu being the leading figure, with Petre Antonescu in close attendance) broke out of their Parisian subservience to create a neo-Romanian style which would gradually infiltrate the urban landscape of Bucharest.

* * * * *

In 1918, in the wake of the First World War, the population of Bucharest was approximately 400,000. This figure would rise to around 1,000,000 by the start of the Second World War. The newer residential districts, such as Dorobanti in the north, expanded accordingly, attracting disparate architectural styles and new aesthetics. During the 1930s, Bucharest decided to modernise itself and opted for a simple and efficient approach to building. Romanian architects were quick to adopt the new architectural compositions, the new formal values of space, in which spatial organisation is strictly subordinated to the functional purposes of the building. Gripped by unprecedented feverishness, the city entered a phase of vertical growth. The new rectangular 'temples' were now built of steel, concrete and glass.

The great boulevards, notably the present-day Maghéru, were laid out in straight lines, and central Bucharest began to turn into a truly modern city. On the old *Calea Victoriei,* American architects built the Telephone Palace (1933), which until the 1970s remained the tallest building in Bucharest.

*19. The MihaiVoda church in 1794: watercolour by W. Watts from L. Mayer.*

*20. The Mihai Voda church and its bell tower: exceptional ecclesiastic monument, built in the purest Byzantine architectonic tradition by the future prince Michael the Brave, 1589.*

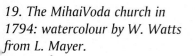

Islands of delightful traditional architecture can still be found almost everywhere in the city, even on the great boulevards.

The 'Little Paris' so loved by Paul Morand existed somewhere – in the heart of the landscape and the souls of its élite.

\* \* \* \* \*

After the Second World War, 'dormitory suburbs' were built around the outskirts of the city. In the 1950s, the huge 'Press House' – an imposed replica of the Lomonosov University in Moscow – was built close to the northern entrance road into the city.

The most astonishing building of the 1980s is the palace built to a North Korean model to satisfy the dream of a megalomaniac communist dictator (the facade is 400 m in length). As well as performing the thankless task of recalling a closed chapter of history, this palace – which was intended to be a symbol of power – has become the city's 'curiosity'.

The surrounding district – the Civic Centre – conceals architectural treasures and jewels of history behind the serried blocks of the great boulevards. Wherever you wander in this quarter you will discover, scattered like mushrooms, monuments which were once key figures in the history of the city and of the country itself, but which now live in a kind of anonymity. Wedged between newer buildings, deprived of their original environment, these monuments seem a little lost and will always remain places of mystery and piety.

Just a few steps away from huge central boulevard of the Civic Centre, Patriarchate Hill (*Dealul Patriarhiei*) proudly retains its beautiful 17th-century church in the Byzantine style, alongside the neo-classical National Assembly Building constructed in 1907.

21. *The drive to Patriarchate Hill.*

22. *Fountain in front of the large Unirea Store.*

23. *The Palace of Justice: French eclectic style – architect Albert Ballu, 1890–1895; 'the waiting room' is designed by architect Ion Mincu.*

24. *Fountain in the Civic Centre.*

Not far away, the Antim Church – founded by the great scholar Antim Ivireanul in the early 18th century – is today the most coherent monastic ensemble in Bucharest, with its enclosing wall, its imposing and exceptionally beautiful *Cuhnia* (kitchen), and its Synodal Palace in the neo-Romanian style.

The lovely church of Domnita Balasa, next to the Palace of Justice on the right bank of the Dâmbovitza, was built by the daughter of the great builder prince Brâncoveanu at the end of the 18th century, and subsequently rebuilt during the 19th century.

23

24

Between the Parliament Palace and the river you will find the church of Mihai Voda, built in 1589 by the future prince Michael the Brave as part of one of the city's first monasteries. In the Byzantine tradition, this exceptional monument features alternate rows of bare and mortared bricks.

Still on the right bank of the Dâmbovitza, not far from Patriarchate Hill, the little 18th-century Bucur Church – whose verandah entrance resembles a peasant house – stands near the church of Radu Voda, which forms part of the city's oldest monastic settlement.

It was surely written in the stars that this city would be more generous than the Destiny which has tested it so harshly with earthquakes, floods, wars, blizzards and interminable droughts. It was written that she would survive it all to fulfil her sacred, primary vocation.

Today, Bucharest has over two million inhabitants, a tenth of the country's overall population.

I have had the opportunity to accompany several westerners, mostly businessmen or journalists, on their first encounters with Bucharest. I have watched with amusement their astonishment and perplexity on discovering the city's contrasts and colours. It was sometimes hard to tell whether they were discouraged or enchanted by what they saw, but in any event they found themselves falling into a different rhythm. Long waits gave them the opportunity to admire the architectural gems surrounding them. Confronted with a magnolia tree in full bloom, they would be spontaneously moved.

After a long evening spent in a jazz club or a tavern with gipsy musicians – where they would almost always find themselves troubled by one of the city's many beautiful women – my new foreign friends would find to their surprise that their carefully-measured western sense of time was no more, that it had been corrupted and eroded by Balkan time with all its imprecision and uncertainty.

25

26

27

*25. The Patriarchal church and the old Chamber of Deputies: the church – built in 1656 by Prince Constantin Serban from a famous post-Byzantine architectonic prototype; the Palace of the Chamber of Deputies – of French eclectic style, architect D. Maimarolu, 1907.*

*26. The Patriarchal church at Easter.*

*27. In the courtyard of the Patriarchal church at Easter.*

*Following pages:*

*28. The Stavropoleos church: night view.*

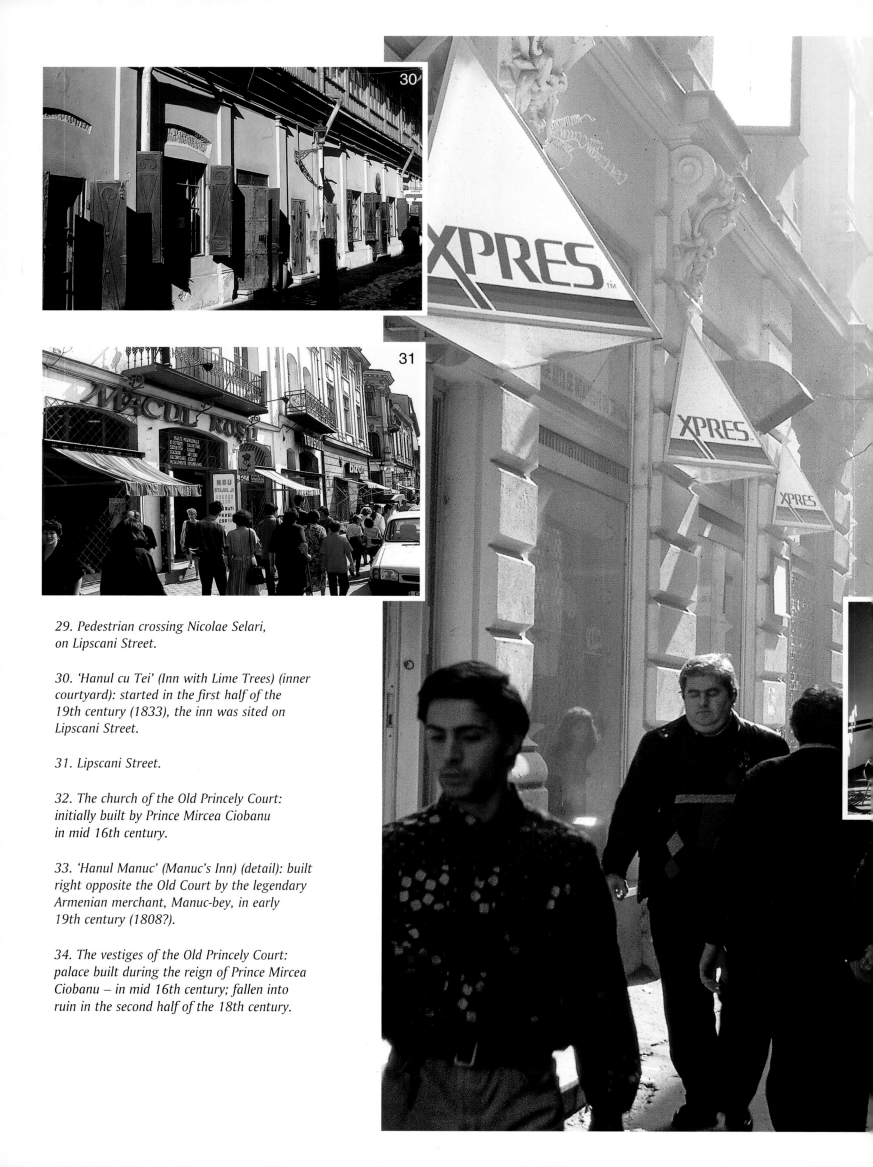

29. Pedestrian crossing Nicolae Selari, on Lipscani Street.

30. 'Hanul cu Tei' (Inn with Lime Trees) (inner courtyard): started in the first half of the 19th century (1833), the inn was sited on Lipscani Street.

31. Lipscani Street.

32. The church of the Old Princely Court: initially built by Prince Mircea Ciobanu in mid 16th century.

33. 'Hanul Manuc' (Manuc's Inn) (detail): built right opposite the Old Court by the legendary Armenian merchant, Manuc-bey, in early 19th century (1808?).

34. The vestiges of the Old Princely Court: palace built during the reign of Prince Mircea Ciobanu – in mid 16th century; fallen into ruin in the second half of the 18th century.

# In the Old Court

Turning off *Calea Victoriei* near the Zlatari Church (the Goldsmiths' Church), we find ourselves on old Lipscani Street. Suddenly we are deep in the very heart of Bucharest's oldest commercial quarter. Its narrow alleys bear the names of the old guilds: *Blanari* (Furriers), *Covaci* (Blacksmiths), *Gabroveni* (from the name given to traders from the Bulgarian town of Gabrovo), *Selari* (Saddlemakers), *Sepcari* (Capmakers). Hundreds of little old shops, perfectly preserved, are crowded together like fragile and frightened creatures clinging to one another for safety. The frenzy of activity is astounding, like a crazy human anthill.

Always a commercial area, the Lipscani quarter grew up gradually on the margin of the Princely Court, here on the gentle hill overlooking the left bank of the Dâmbovitza. The surviving traces of this Old Court include the ruins of the prince's palace and – in particular – a beautiful and harmoniously proportioned post-Byzantine church dating from the 16th century.

32

Since we are so close to the Princely Court, we might pause opposite it to take a cup of Turkish coffee in the inner garden of the *Hanul Manuc* inn, savouring the oriental aroma and the peace of this place where the spirit of the Armenian merchant adventurer Manuc-bey still lingers.

To prolong the flavour of those times, we might take a last look at the Galerie des Halles – an old building from the 19th century just behind the inn, the haunt of antique dealers and second hand booksellers – and the art 'treasures' in the *Hanul cu Tei* ('Lime-Tree Inn') halfway along Lipscani Street.

The quarter has been filled with this vitality for centuries. Once the country entered the modern era, the flourishing trade needed banking services, and imposing edifices housing financial institutions began to mark out their territory.

Lipscani Street attracted numerous banking establishments, including the Romanian National Bank (1883) and the Commercial Stock Exchange – now the National Library – (1910), both built in the French neo-classical style, and the neo-Romanian Marmoroschblank (1915–1923).

At the side of the University Square, the offices of the General Insurance Company (now the Romanian Commercial Bank) were erected in 1906.

The buildings of two financial companies of the inter-war period, 'Adriatica' and 'Agricola Fonciera', line *Calea Victoriei* before it comes to a halt on the banks of the Dâmbovitza.

Immediately opposite, on the right bank, sits a little Syrian church over two hundred years old, risen from its ashes and seeming to scoff at all atheistic pretensions: the church of St Spiridon the Elder was demolished in 1987, only to be rebuilt by the Patriarchate to the original design in 1995. A little further along on the same bank is the Palace of Justice, built in the French neo-Renaissance style of the late 19th century.

35. *The Baratia church: mentioned for the first time in 1578; rebuilt in 1847.*

36. *The St Gheorghe Nou church: built in late 17th century; the great Prince Constantin Brâncoveanu is buried here and his statue is by sculptor Oscar Han (1939).*

36

35

37. *The big brasserie Carul cu Bere (interior view): eclectic style, mainly neo-gothic – architect Zigfrid Kofzinsky (1875).*

37

38. The Russian church (bell towers): built between 1905 and 1909.

39. The Romanian National Bank (B.N.R.): French eclectic style –
architects Albert Galleron, Cassien Bernard, 1883–1885.

40. The Romanian Bank for Development (B.R.D.) (formerly Marmoroschblank):
mainly neo-romanian style – architect Petre Antonescu, 1915–1923.

39

40

41. Bucharest Financial Plazza.

42. Bucharest Financial Plazza (detail).

43. The National Library (formerly Chamber of Commerce)
(detail): French eclectic style – architect St Burcus, 1910.

44. 'Strada Halelor' (Covered Market Street): between the left bank of the Dâmbovitza and the Old Princely Court district.

45. The Dâmbovitza river bend: at the level of the Independence Quai 'Splaiul Independentei'.

46. 'Galeria Halelor' (Covered Market Gallery): booksellers, second-hand booksellers and antique dealers, not far from the Old Princely Court, in a late 19th century building.

47

*47. United Nations Square (formerly Senate Square): in the background, the two buildings of the former financial companies, Agricola (1928) and Adriatica (1930) – architect Petre Antonescu.*

*48. The Savings Bank (C.E.C.) and the Romanian History Museum (view from above).*

*49. The Savings Bank (C.E.C.) (interior view).*

The old *Calea Victoriei* (Victory Avenue) is the perfect balm for a troubled or disillusioned soul.

This extraordinary, paradoxical avenue is the most spectacular place, crammed with an astonishing variety of buildings. It is impossible to tire of wandering along this street lined with houses and magnificent palaces, taverns and high-class shops, banks and museums.

The eye lingers on the shop-windows and the slim, swaying silhouettes of women. The walls emanate the delicate white light of the southern afternoon. The tavern proprietors have placed two or three small tables on the pavement, and opened parasols whose fringes are stirred by a light breeze. The traffic moves scarcely faster than the crowds of people.

As soon as it leaves the Dâmbovitza river, brushing the edge of the Old Court, *Calea Victoriei* sets out on its old princely course, opening itself to the light and the grand buildings in attendance, such as the old Post Office Palace (now the National History Museum) and the Savings and Deposit Bank, both built in the characteristically eclectic Belle Epoque style.

Narrowing for a while, *Calea Victoriei* climbs up to the crossroads of the Officers' Club, which is built in the French neo-classical style. Immediately opposite is the 'Capsa House' *(Casa Capsa)*, a hotel-cum-restaurant-cum-brasserie opened in 1868 by a former student of a celebrated Parisian confectioner. In just a few years, the Capsa earned an envied reputation as Bucharest's favourite rendezvous, and for over a century has enjoyed a status similar to that of La Coupole, the famous Paris café. Its clientele has included many Romanian and foreign celebrities. The French writer Paul Morand, who fell passionately in love with Bucharest (his wife, Helene Chrisoveloni, was Romanian), wrote a book entitled *Bucharest* (1935) in which he describes wonderfully the complicated history and ambiguous fate of this city. For him, the Capsa House was 'the heart of the city, the drum of the giant ear that is Bucharest'.

48

*50. The St Spiridon Vechi church: Syrian church, erected in 1747 during the phanariote reign of Constantin Mavrocordat and consecrated to the Antioche patriarchate; the church was demolished in 1987 and reconstructed in 1995 through the good offices of the Church.*

*51. The Savings Bank (C.E.C.), night view: French eclectic style – architect Paul Gottereau, 1896–1900.*

*52. The Romanian History Museum (formerly Post Office Palace) (detail): French eclectic style – architect Al. Savulescu 1894–1900.*

50

51

Here, as at the next crossroads, the warm colours of huge baskets of flowers lend an elegant air to the street. Bucharest's flowersellers, who can be found at most of the city's crossroads, set up their wares every day come rain or shine, as they have done for over a hundred years. Reminiscent of characters from some operetta, rather quaint and picturesque, they are a simple, unpretentious symbol of this city.

As we continue our stroll, the street narrows again and we find ourselves on a parade of high-class shops, with the tall buildings packed so close together that in some places the daylight scarcely seems to reach the ground.

Suddenly the street widens as we enter Revolution Square (formerly Royal Palace Square), a site steeped in history. The disparate architectural styles of the surrounding buildings blend together very harmoniously and naturally: the old Royal Palace, built in the inter-war period and now housing the well-endowed Art Museum in one of its wings, the University Library in the late 19th-century 'Beaux Arts' style, a cubist hotel (the Hilton, formerly the Athénée Palace) and a beautiful 18th-century church (the Cretulescu).

It was here in this square that the movement which led to the collapse of the communist dictatorship found its impetus.

In front of the auditorium of the Romanian Athenaeum, *Calea Victoriei* widens further still to form a square. The auditorium, an eclectic architectural gem of the late 19th century, is topped by a dome 41 metres in height and resembles a Greek temple. A curious fact: its old foundations were originally intended for the construction of a merry-go-round. In the square of the Athenaeum there is a bronze statue of the greatest of Romanian poets, Mihai Eminescu, created by the sculptor Gheorghe Anghel.

Narrowing once again as it leaves Palace Square, now lined with luxury hotels, elegant houses (Monteoru and Vernescu), magnificent palaces (Cantacuzino), this 'royal road' ends its meandering course in Victory Square *(Piata Victoriei),* where it meets its great rival the Maghéru-Catargiu Boulevard.

52

53. *The National Military Circle: French eclectic style – architects Dimitrie Maimarolu, Ernest Doneaud, 1912.*

54. *The Zlatari (Goldsmiths) church: initially erected by Prince Matei Basarab in the first half of the 17th century; rebuilt in 1850.*

55. *The National Military Circle (interior view).*

56. *Flower merchants on 'Calea Victoriei' (Victory Avenue).*

57. *'Calea Victoriei' (view from above) between the Capsa House and the Telephone Palace.*

58. 'Calea Victoriei': the most famous avenue in Bucharest, between the Capsa House (1868) and the Telephone Palace (1933).

59. The Continental Hotel (formerly Elias), night view: German eclectic style – architect Rittern Forster, 1886.

61

62

63

*Preceding pages:*

*60. The Romanian National Art Museum (interior view).*

*61. The University Library (formerly Carol the Ist University Foundation): French eclectic style – architect Paul Gottereau, 1891–1895; finished in 1914.*

*62. The Romanian National Art Museum: a wing of the Royal Palace, a building reconstructed in its present form according to plans drawn up by architect N. Neciulescu, 1930.*

*63. The Kretzulescu church: built in 1722 by the son-in-law and daughter of the late Prince Constantin Brâncoveanu, restored in 1935–1936; the founders' portraits are painted by Gheorghe Tattarescu, a 19th century Romanian painter.*

65

*64. The Romanian Athenaeum: auditorium of French eclectic style with a neo-classical facade – architect Albert Galleron, 1886–1888; in front of the Athenaeum, the statue of the great Romanian 19th century poet, Mihai Eminescu (sculptor Gheorghe Anghel).*

*65. The Hilton Hotel (formerly Athénée Palace), night view: initially built in 1912 – architect Théophile Bradeau; rebuilt in 1937 by architect Duiliu Marcu; restored several times.*

*66. St Joseph's Cathedral: built by architect Frederic Schmidt, 1873–1884.*

*67. The Stirbey Palace (presently the Museum of Ceramics and Porcelain): built in 1837 by architect Michel St Jourand; rebuilt in neo-classic style – architect F. Hartmann, 1881.*

*68. The Art Collections Museum (formerly Romanit Palace): 1883.*

**66**

**67**

**68**

*69. The Monteoru House (today the Writers' House) (interior view): rebuilt in its present form by architect Ion Mincu, 1887–1889.*

*70. The Vernescu House (today a casino) (interior view): rebuilt in its present form by architect Ion Minc,1887; interior paintings by G.D. Mirea.*

*71. The Cantacuzino Palace (today a Museum of Romanian Music): eclectic style with elements of Art Nouveau – architect I. D. Berindey, 1898–1900.*

*72. The Cantacuzino Palace (interior view).*

# Centrum mundi

The city's first real boulevard was laid in 1855, alongside the land earmarked for the building of the University. Subsequently, as we have already noted, the road was progressively extended both eastwards and westwards to become one of the three great historic axes of the city (along with *Calea Victoriei* and the Maghéru Boulevard).

Construction of the University began in 1857 and was completed in the following decade, but building work was to be resumed repeatedly in the early 20th century as new faculties were added. The imposing edifice behind the University is the School of Architecture, built in the neo-Romanian style.

In front of the University is a hexagonal square. Here you will find a series of statues depicting cultural and historical personages such as Michael the Brave, seen here on horseback. This statue, created by Carrier-Belleuse in 1876, is the finest of its kind in Bucharest.

Two spectacular 19th-century buildings – the Ministry of Agriculture, in the French neo-Renaissance style, and the Museum of the History of the City of Bucharest (Sutu Palace, 1834) – border the southern corner of the University crossroads.

In the early 1970s, the Intercontinental Hotel was erected at the end of the Maghéru Boulevard. This is the tallest building in the city, with over twenty storeys. Beside it is the imposing ensemble of the National Theatre, which houses several concert halls and exhibition rooms, a jazz club (the *Laptaria lui Enache*) and a terrace bar (the *Motor*), all of which are popular meeting-places for young people and artists. An International Book Fair is held here in June every year.

73. The University crossroads: from left to right – the University, the Intercontinental Hotel and the National Theatre.

74. The University: initially built between 1857 and 1869 by architect Alexandru Orascu; subsequently enlarged in several stages according to plans drawn up by architect N. Ghika-Budesti.

75. The statue of Prince Michael the Brave, erected by sculptor Carrier Belleuze, 1876.

76. The Romanian Commercial Bank (B.C.R.) (formerly the office of the General Insurance Company), night view: built between 1897 and 1914 according to plans drawn up by architect O. Maugsch.

77. Second hand booksellers on the steps of the University.

79

80

81

82

*Preceding pages:*

*78. The Sutu Palace (today Museum of the History of the City of Bucharest): built between 1832 and 1834 by Konrad Schwing.*

*79. The Coltea church and hospital: church of 'brâncovenesc' style, built in 1704 by boyar Mihai Cantacuzino; closely related to the oldest hospital in Bucharest.*

*80. The Ministry of Agriculture: French eclectic style – architect Louis Blanc, 1896.*

*81. The Intercontinental Hotel (entrance) and a wing of the National Theatre, night view: the hotel – architects D. Hariton, Gh. Nadrag, I. Moscu, R. Belea, 1970–1971; the theatre – architects H. Maicu, R. Belea, N. Cucu, 1967–1970; subsequently modified.*

*82. Students selling Easter cards in front of the University.*

*83. The 'Dintr-o zi' (In one day) church: erected in 1702 by Marica Doamna, wife of Prince Constantin Brâncoveanu.*

*84. The School of Architecture: neo-romanian style – architect Grigore Cerchez, 1912–1927*

# Wandering westwards and some east side pictures

If you want to sample the beauty of Bucharest at a leisurely pace on foot, the Kogalniceanu Boulevard and the Cotroceni quarter offer some of the most rewarding adventures.

86

Starting from University Square and heading towards the Opera House, the Kogalniceanu Boulevard leads us peacefully through the sea of people to the Officers' Club, at the crossroads with the legendary *Calea Victoriei*.

A little further along, there is a welcoming cluster of restaurants and cinemas occupying the ground floors of multi-storey buildings in the French style of the early years of this century. The pavements are narrow. Little street-sellers hawk their wares half-heartedly. The hustle and bustle of the street seems to take you hostage, but it is an amicable uproar full of laughter which does not abate until late in the night.

Continuing our stroll westwards, immediately opposite the neo-Romanian City Hall (*Primaria*) we find the Cismigiu, Bucharest's oldest park.

The Cismigiu is a very popular place, pleasantly situated alongside the main east–west road. It is a place where you can find a little peace and composure right in the very heart of the city's busiest quarter.

Designed in the mid-19th century by an Austrian landscape gardener, and subsequently extended and modified by a German architect, Cismigiu Park is often said to be reminiscent of Parisian gardens such as the Jardin des Plantes or the Parc Monceau.

*85. The Ministry of Justice (formerly palace of the Association of Veterinary Surgeons): built between 1929 and 1932 according to plans drawn up by architect Constantin Jotzu.*

*86. The City Hall of Bucharest 'Primaria Capitalei': neo-romanian style – architect Petre Antonescu, 1906–1910.*

Cismigiu Park is the emotional and aesthetic heart of Bucharest, where lovers exchange endless kisses under the gaze of the old people sitting in the shade of the trees and shrubs laid out in ingenious and exotic arrangements; where those thirsty for peace and colour may find a little quiet contemplation in its secret nooks and crannies.

87

88

89

It is also a place of great human variety, where the city's inhabitants come to watch the world go by. Cismigiu is a little of everything: a crèche for young children, a refuge for truant schoolboys, a home for the homeless, an open-air public library, a meeting-place for football fans and chess players, and a 'summer garden' (terrace restaurant).

During the winter holidays, the park is transformed into an exuberant 'children's village'. The Romanians are extremely fond of this – a kind of merry, brightly-coloured Disneyland, where the show goes on for weeks at a time.

\* \* \* \* \*

After passing the Law School, built between the wars – facing the Opera House on the opposite bank of the Dâmbovitza – we enter the magnificent, elegant and exuberant Cotroceni quarter, which is largely inhabited by artists, doctors and academics. A residential area full of 'villas' (detached houses) built in the early years of this century, Cotroceni is perhaps the most vibrant quarter of the city. Swathed in greenery, surrounded and dotted with little parks, cut across by large streets, Cotroceni bubbles with life, youth and music.

\* \* \* \* \*

On Cotroceni Hill, at the end of the boulevard which bisects the quarter, stands the cold figure of the Military Academy (the 'School of War', built between the wars).

Just a short walk away is the Botanical Garden – an impressive collection of plants and trees of all kinds, surrounded by lakes and hills. Its neighbours are the Cotroceni Palace, built on the site of an old monastic settlement, and the School of Medicine, which dates from 1902 and is one of Bucharest's oldest university establishments.

*87. Cismigiu Gardens: inaugurated in 1845 during the reign of Barbu Stirbey – conceived by the German landscape gardener F.W. Mayer.*

*88–90. Cismigiu Gardens.*

*91. The Law School: built in 1935 by architect Petre Antonescu.*

*92. The Kretzulescu Palace (housing today the headquarters of UNESCO): French eclectic style – architect Petre Antonescu, 1914.*

90

91

92

93

94

95

93. The Medical Faculty: French eclectic style – architect Louis Blanc, 1903.

94. St Elefterie Vechi church: built in 1747.

95. The Romanian Opera: built 1952–1953 by architect Octav Doicescu.

96, 97. Houses (villas) in the Cotroceni district.

96

97

98

98. The Military Academy (formerly School of War):
built in 1939 by architect Duiliu Marcu .

99. The Botanical Gardens – planted in 1892
on the Cotroceni Hill, on the initiative of
Professor Dimitrie Brandza.

100. The monument of the Engineers Heroes (Leul):
erected by sculptor Spiridon Georgescu in 1926.

99

SPUNEȚI
GENERAȚIILOR VIITOARE
CĂ NOI AM FĂCUT SUPREMA JERTFĂ
PE CÂMPURILE DE BĂTAIE
PENTRU ÎNTREGIREA NEAMULUI

101

102

104

101. *The Armenian church: 17th century monument; entirely reconstructed in 1911 according to plans drawn up by architect Dimitrie Maimarolu (inspired by the Echimiadziu cathedral in Erevan).*

102. *The Rosetti Square: in the middle – the statue of the 19th century politician and writer C.A. Rosetti (erected in 1903 by the sculptor W.C. Hegel).*

103. *The Greek church: shaped as an antique Greek temple (about 1900).*

104. *The Bellfry 'Foisorul de Foc' (presently the Firemen Museum): built in 1893.*

105

107

108

105. *The National College (Cantemir Voda): old 19th century gymnasium, rebuilt in 1915.*

106. *The Darvari Priory church: built in 1869; at that time subordinated to a monastery of the Athos Mountain.*

107. *The Assan Palace (today House of the Scientists – C.O.S.): built in 1914 by architect I.D. Berindey.*

108. *House on the Luca Stroici Street.*

109. *The Circus Park: the Circus building was put up in 1960 by architects N. Porumbescu, C. Rulea and N. Pruncu.*

# On the Maghéru Boulevard

The Maghéru Boulevard was first laid in the last century, but it acquired its present appearance between the wars, when its pavements were straightened and impressive rectangular buildings were constructed along its length. The Ambassador Hotel dates from this period, as does the ARO building, whose great hall – extremely well furnished for its time – hosted concerts by Enescu and Casals before the Second World War, as well as the most prestigious exhibitions. The Maghéru is the busiest of Bucharest's boulevards, with young people constantly coming and going between the University and the School of Architecture at one end and the Academy of Higher Economic Studies (built in the 1920s) at the other. Second only to the historic city centre, this boulevard also has the highest concentration of services such as travel agencies, bureaux de change, luxury hotels and restaurants, cinemas and bookshops such as the elegant Dalles Hall, not far from the University.

*110. The bookshop in the Dalles Hall.*

*111. The Maghéru Boulevard: the main north–south road of the city.*

*112. The Italian church: built 1911–1915 by architect Mario Stoppa.*

*113. The Théodor Aman Museum (interior view): built in 1869 according to plans drawn up by the 19th century painter, Théodor Aman.*

People go walking '*pe Maghéru*' (on the Maghéru) for the simple pleasure of it, just as they do on the Champs Elysées in Paris. If you stroll between University Square and Romana Square (*Piata Romana*) several times in a day, you are likely to encounter the same handsome Wallachian silhouettes again and again.

Abandoning its straight course just before it changes name and direction, the boulevard widens into Romana Square. Here there is a statue of the Roman she-wolf – '*Lupoaica*' ('Lupa Capitolina' in Latin) – symbolising the Latin people, a gift from the city of Rome in 1906.

114. The Lido Hotel: initally built in the 30s — architect E. Doneaud, recently restored.

115. The Ambasador Hotel: built in the 30s according to plans drawn up by architect Arghir Culina.

116. 'Lupoaica' (the She-wolf): statue offered in 1906 to the city of Bucharest by the city of Rome as a token of latinity; presently located in Piata Romana.

117. Queuing in front of the cinema of the ARO building.

118. The Academy of Economic Studies (A.S.E): neo-classic style — architect Van Saanen, 1926.

116

117

118

119

120

119. The Storck Museum:
hosting works by sculptor
Franz Storck and his wife
Cecilia Cutescu – architect
A. Clavel, 1913.

120. Boulevard Lascar
Catargiu: the northward
continuation of Boulevard
Maghéru.

121.The Storck Museum
(interior view).

# 'Walking the *Sosea*'

The Maghéru Boulevard offers the promise of coolness among the lakes and parks to the north of the city when the scorching heat of August melts the asphalt. The lakes providing the city with its northern protection are actually named as ponds – *Herastrau*, the pond of flowers – *Floreasca*, the pond of trees – *Tei*, and so on.

*122. Victory Square 'Piata Victoriei' (view from above): the buildings of the Romanian Peasant Museum, the Institute of Geology and the Victoria Palace can be seen.*

*123. The Grigore Antipa Museum of Natural History: built in 1906.*

A stroll in the parkland around the Herastrau is rather like an evening at a concert hall. This is a vast park, with broad paths and perfectly tended flower-beds. The statues, little colonnades, elegant footbridges and weeping willows around the margin of the lake make for a pleasantly serene atmosphere.

But this is not the only reason for the pilgrimage by the city's inhabitants, who visit mainly at weekends. Strolling here is rooted in an old tradition of the city which dates back to the last century: 'walking the path' (the 'Sosea').

Once a favoured pastime of the rich with their coaches and limousines, 'walking the Sosea' is now within everyone's reach. However, it still retains its elegance and style, and something of the glittering, aristocratic aura of days gone by. To reach Herastrau Park from the city centre, take either Kisseleff Avenue (*Soseaua Kisseleff*) or Aviators' Boulevard (*Bulevardul Aviatorilor*).

\* \* \* \* \*

There is one last frontier to cross before you reach the park: the Dorobanti-Domeni quarter. This is a rather refined area, where most people would like to live if they were given the choice.

If 'arrogance' is the single word that springs to mind when I walk rather timidly through the nearby Primaverii quarter, 'discretion' is the word I find myself murmuring when I allow myself to be carried along by the scent of the lime-trees in this residential area.

The Dorobanti quarter is crossed by several great boulevards, including Dorobanti Street (*Calea Dorobanti*), Aviators' Boulevard (*Bulevardul Aviatorilor*) and Kisseleff Avenue, which link the city centre with the northern entrance roads. If you turn off these boulevards, you will be greeted by the welcoming calm of little streets and lanes thick with trees and flower-beds, and will be quickly rewarded by the charm of the ivy-covered houses. Every house breathes imagination and elegance (each has its own little yard, its garden with fences low enough to allow a nosy peek). Their original owners were cultivated people who enjoyed life and the visits of friends; well-off people who, in the early years of the century, demanded not only talent from their architects but also originality. The results transformed the quarter – in some ways quite rambling, and yet compact, like a complete little town in itself – into a spectacular architectural exhibition of great variety.

* * * * *

The Primaverii residential quarter lies at the entrance to Herastrau Park, on the edge of Floreasca Lake. Not so long ago, one of the streets here was completely closed off. Lined with trees and flowers, it was blocked with iron gates guarded by policemen and dogs, forming a barricade for the great 'villas', veritable fortresses which were supposed to protect the senior dignitaries of the Communist Party.

* * * * *

Since you came out to 'walk the path', it would surely be a pity to miss two of the most interesting museums in Romania: the Romanian Peasant Museum and the Village Museum.

The old Romanian civilisation has produced a rich and colourful folk culture, indeed one of the most original peasant cultures in Europe. Still intact in more remote areas, but declining in most parts of the country, the mythology and peasant traditions of the Carpathians and the Danube can be discovered by visiting these museums.

The Romanian Peasant Museum is housed in a grand neo-Romanian building situated at the crossroads of Victory Square and Kisseleff Avenue. In mid-June every year, the Music Festival offers a wonderful pageant of folklore in the living setting of a real peasant fair.

Built on the western edge of Herastrau Lake in 1936 as part of the celebration of 'Bucharest Month', the Village Museum is constantly enriched. It brings together in the open air all types of Romanian peasant architecture, and is among the most celebrated of its kind anywhere in the world. In summer and during festivals, the Museum puts on numerous folkloric events at which craftsmen from all parts of Romania work in clay, wood or fabrics, watched by fascinated onlookers.

Right beside the museum – at the junction of several radial roads including Kisseleff Avenue – stands a symbol of the Bucharest people's taste for heterogeneity: the granite Triumphal Arch. Also built in 1936 (following vigorous lobbying by the composer George Enescu, among others), the Arch replaced a temporary wood and stucco monument.

In the same year, Kisseleff Avenue was extended beyond the Triumphal Arch, running past Herastrau Park and the Village Museum towards Baneasa Station and Baneasa Airport, both built between the wars.

Beyond the airport, the Baneasa Woods bring us the perfume of the centuries-old forests which once surrounded the city.

124

125

*124. The Romanian Peasant Museum (formerly National Art Museum): neo-romanian style – architect N. Ghika-Budesti, 1912–1939.*

*125. The Romanian Peasant Museum (interior view).*

*126. The Institute of Geology: neo-romanian style – architect Victor Stefanescu, 1906.*

*127. The Victoria Palace (today the Government's headquarters): built in 1937 by architect D. Marcu.*

128. *Residential area at 'Sosea'.*

129. *The Bistro 'Bufetul' from 'Sosea': neo-romanian style – architect Ion Mincu, 1889–1892.*

130. *Residential area at 'Sosea'.*

131. *'Piata Aviatorilor' (Pilots' Square), night view: in the middle, 'Crucea Secolului' (the Cross of the Century), by sculptor Paul Neagu, 1997.*

**129**

**130**

**131**

134

135

132. The large Herastrau Park: in the background, the House of the Free Press (formerly Casa Scanteii), built in the 50s.

133, 134. The large Herastrau Park.

135. The Triumphal Arch: erected in 1935–1936 by architect Petre Antonescu.

136. Terrace-restaurant on the Herastrau Lake.

136

138

139

*Preceding pages:*

*137. The Casin church (former church of the Domeni Park): built in 1937 – architect D. Ionescu Berechet.*

*138. Religious wedding at the Casin church.*

*139. Easter at the Casin church.*

*140. Beautiful Wallachian girls…*

*141. World Trade Centre: architects V. Vion, N.Taralunga, 1993–1994.*

*142. Young girls in town.*

143. *The Village Museu m: set up on the initiative of sociologist Dimitrie Gusti, inaugurated in 1936; steadily developed and enlarged.*

Strolling around Bucharest, you will inevitably come across one of its great markets ('*piata*' in Romanian).

Like everyone else in Bucharest, I often go to the market – and not necessarily to do any shopping. There is an evocative Romanian expression, '*a face piata*' (literally 'to do the market'), which suggests the encounter with a colourful universe, an extraordinary spectacle bringing together all manner of people and objects.

145

There are various types of market in Bucharest, some of which have retained the appearance, if not necessarily the name, of the '*Hala*' (covered market) with its distinctive architecture so characteristic of the Parisian Belle Epoque (*Halele Obor*, *Hala Traian*). The elegant and expensive *Amzei* market is situated in the city centre, between *Calea Victoriei* and the Maghéru Boulevard. Next to the North Station, you will find the popular *Buzesti* market, which has kept its old name of *Matache Macelaru* ('Matache the Butcher').

But the 'real' market is the *Obor* (meaning 'fair') in the eastern part of the city. As big as a small village, the market has hundreds of stalls, kiosks, stands, booths and cellars. It is a magnificent spectacle: mountains of fruit and vegetables, pens full of livestock, thousands of people loudly selling their wares with colourful and tempting patter.

146

At the great *Obor* market you will find more than just fruit, vegetables, cheese and livestock. Everything that can possibly be sold or bought is laid out on hundreds of stalls: huge bales of wool, secondhand clothes, 'naïve' paintings, fishing rods, cage-birds, artificial flowers, pottery, hundreds of barrels of pickled vegetables.

The huge *talcioc* (flea market) occupying one end of the market brings together all the curiosities of the half-urban, half-peasant universe of Bucharest.

144, 145. *At the market…*

146. *At the flea market…*

147. *The North Station: inaugurated at the same time as the main Bucharest–Ploiesti railway, in 1872; the Grivita wing, of neo-classic style, was drawn up by architect Victor Stefanescu.*

148. *Underground station: the first Bucharest underground station was commissioned in 1979.*

149. *Bus stop in a 'dormitory suburb'.*

150. The 'Bucharest 1900 Carnival' at the old Princely Court.

151. The 'Bucharest 1900 Carnival' in the old Covaci Street (Blacksmiths Street).

152. 'Mici'-merchant at the 'Bucharest 1900 Carnival'.

153. Street musicians.

152

# Urban festivals

Every year, in late May and early June, Bucharest dresses itself up in the clothing of the Belle Epoque and speaks the language of that era. Between the Old Court and *Calea Victoriei* there are performances, parades, allegorical

floats, and plenty of '*mici*' and beer, making for a very special atmosphere, both nostalgic and picturesque. The *Bucharest 1900* carnival lasts for three days and three crazy nights.

\* \* \* \* \*

You shouldn't be surprised. Theatre is to the people of Bucharest what Opera is to the Italians: it preoccupies them, obsesses them, nourishes them. It is a vital necessity.

During the last years of the communist regime, theatre meant everything to the Romanian people. It was their newspaper, television, commentary, platform and escape route.

Theatre has retained its central position and is extraordinarily popular; every first night is a special occasion. There are numerous schools of dramatic art and production. There are even itinerant players, as well as experimental theatres, comedy theatres and street theatres. Romanian directors are always given a warm welcome in other countries.

\* \* \* \* \*

In September every year, the Georges Enesco Music Festival is held in Bucharest. Many famous musicians have appeared on the stages of the Athenaeum, the Palace Hall and the Radio House: Menuhin (the disciple of the great Romanian composer George Enesco), Rostropovich, Richter and many others.

# Evening shadows

Bucharest also has casinos (some of which are housed very grandly in great palaces), smart or informal nightclubs, and restaurants to satisfy every taste.

If you want to make merry, you could choose a tavern with a little gipsy orchestra ('*taraf*'), or you might like to try the '*mici*' (a kind of sausage made with a mixture of meats) with a jug of wine. You might even sing, if your heart moves you. You will find taverns like these all over the city.

Particularly in the autumn, during the grape harvest, restaurants serving traditional Romanian cuisine are easily recognised by the reed fences surrounding them. This is the certain sign of a '*mustarie*', where you can drink fresh or mildly fermented grape juice (called '*must*' or '*tulburel*' – rough wine) and eat '*pastrama*' (pastrami made from dried, salted mutton).

'*Gradina de vara*' (summer garden) is the Romanian term for the terrace restaurants which are so popular during the long hot season. Whether it be a grand city-centre or lakeside restaurant, or a small local tavern spilling over on to the pavement, the summer garden is a central feature of the Bucharest landscape. In accordance with time-honoured gastronomic tradition, you will be offered aubergine caviar with fried sweet peppers, '*branza*' (a peasant cheese steeped in brine) and olives; '*mamaliga*' (polenta) with mild cheese and fresh cream, and the famous steaks – gigantic and delicious – which have always been the pride of Bucharest. The custom is to wash everything down with a well-chilled, dry white wine.

If you were unaware of Romania's status as a wine-growing country – it is one of the world's top ten growers – you should visit the Bucharest Wine Fair in mid-April. For three days, dozens of Romanian vineyards present an authentic and quite astonishing oenological culture.

*154. Terrace-restaurant on Lipscani Street.*

*155. Interior view of a cafe.*

*156. The big brasserie Carul cu Bere (interior view): eclectic style, mainly neo-gothic – architect Zigfrid Kofzinsky (1875).*

157. The Caldarusani monastery: built in 1638 by Prince Matei Basarab in order to protect Bucharest.

158. The church of the Plumbuita monastery: monastic ensemble built 1556–1568 by the Wallachian prince Peter the Great and his mother, Doamna Chiajna; the first printing shop in Bucharest was set up here in 1582.

159. The church of the Cernica monastery: built in 1608 by the boyar Cernica.

160. The Cernica monastery on the Cernica Lake.

159

158

# The surrounding area

All around Bucharest, less than an hour's drive through picturesque villages, you can find monasteries, palaces and magnificent old manors on the edges of wide, clear lakes or in the middle of ancient forests of oaks and limes. Mostly built in the 16th and 17th centuries on the pattern of the fortified Byzantine monastery – a small church circled by a thick walled enclosure housing the monks' cells – the orthodox monasteries perfectly evoke the old Bucharest and the means by which it lived and breathed in the days of the founder-princes, protectors of the Christian world.

The Plumbuita monastery now finds itself virtually within the city perimeter, on the edge of Tei Lake.

Just a few kilometres to the east, the Pasarea and Cernica monasteries are reflected in the lakes of the same names, as is the Comana monastery some thirty kilometres to the south.

A similar distance to the north, the Caldarusani monastery was founded by the great builder prince Matei Basarab. A few kilometres away is the Snagov monastery; legend has it that the plunder of Vlad the Impaler is buried in its grounds.

These monasteries have always been places of prayer and culture. A tourist industry has developed around them, because they are also places of pilgrimage for the inhabitants of Bucharest during religious holidays.

However, the most spectacular site in the environs of Bucharest must be the palace built around 1700 by Prince Constantin Brâncoveanu. Lying 14 kilometres north-west of Bucharest, on the edge of a lake carpeted with water-lilies, the Mogosoaia Palace is one of the most magnificent jewels of Wallachian architecture.

160

161

162

*161. The Mogosoaia Palace: architectonic jewel of the early 18th century, residence of the great Prince Constantin Brâncoveanu; restored by the Venetian architect Rupola at the request of the Romanian writer of French language, Marthe Bibesco.*

*162. The Mogosoaia Palace and its ensemble (detail of the inner courtyard).*

*163. The Pasarea monastery on the Pasarea Lake: nunnery built in 1813.*

**Publishing Director:** Jean-Paul Manzo

**Edited by:** Radu Lungu

**Text:** Radu Anton Roman and Radu Lungu

**Captions:** Mihai Petru Georgescu

**Art direction:** Parkstone Press Ltd

**Typesetting:** Karin Erskine

**Photo sources:** Dan Ioan Dinescu, Mircea Savu

**Thanks to:** Fondation ARTEXPO for the pictures of the 1930s

Parkstone Press Ltd
Printed and bound in Europe, 1999
ISBN 1 85995 597 5